# RIVER STONE

## A Collection of Poems

# RIVER STONE

## A Collection of Poems

# KAREN HAYES

McCAA BOOKS • SANTA ROSA

McCaa Books

McCaa Books
1604 Deer Run
Santa Rosa, CA 95405

ISBN 978-0-692-80360-8

First published in 2017 by McCaa Books,
an imprint of McCaa Publications.

Printed in the United States of America
Set in Minion Pro

Cover photograph by Karen Hayes.

Cover design and book layout by Waights Taylor Jr.

www.mccaabooks.com

*Dedication*

*To my mother, Isabel J. Barry Hayes Stevens,*
*who may not always follow through*
*but Always perseveres --*
*and my sister Cherry*
*who always asks if I'm still writing*
*Yes*


*A special Thank You to Waights Taylor, Jr.*
*who, in the midst of a mundane conversation at a book event,*
*astounded me by saying "I'd like to…"*
*and so this book came together.*
*I have no idea why.*

# CONTENTS

## *Preface*

THIS IS THE FIRST COLLECTION OF POEMS published by a new voice and is not likely to be her last. Written in a sparse, tight style, Karen Hayes describes life and her observations in a striking and haunting way, sure to make a reader pause and reflect.

Tonight, in the infinitesimal light of the stars,
The trees and the flowers have been strewing their cool odors.
I walk among them, but none of them are noticing.

*Sylvia Plath*

## Poking

Poking refuse
with a stick
seeing what comes out
or tries to hide

I'll grab its tail
and run with it
screaming
through the alley
down the streets

Follow where it goes
not having any idea
what sort of trip
it'll take me on
or where
we'll end up
after the flight
the struggle

Hoping
there will be enough light left
to make my way
back home

## River Stone

I hold in my hand
a stone from your river
Where one night
words were flung
into the current of time
Where one evening
voices mingled
with scents from the garden
Where there was talk of dams   and summer water   and trees
Where there was talk of wine   and cheese   and chickens
Where the food was simple   and complex
    like the people gathered
    and the poetry spoken to the dark sky
Where a duet of English and Spanish mingled
Where conversation brought possibilities
    and a trickle of belief
I try to hold your words
      like catching raindrops in fog
I try to hold your words

I hold in my hand
a stone from my river

### Broken Chair

I have seen
the mask come off
in the dark of night
under stars and moon
Savage primal
returning
determined to be
in that moment
nothing but madness
Lunar light
the only observer
to inexpressible rage
of defeat
and loss
Rational reason
hurled aside
like those pieces of chair
now fit
only for kindling
Howls erupt
strangled    stifled
transparent in the sky

## Glass Bead

Cool glacier lake
in the palm of my hand
Blue blob of molten
like love    like midnight
rising like daisies
on my windowsill,
silent in the manner of flowers

I hear kettledrums
as the stars in this crystal glimmer
with the sun
balanced on my finger

My touch is smooth as broken glass
piercing as the echoes made when I
hold you
against my heart
strings move and sway with the aroma
of musk and damp dog

I taste autumn leaves
mud and music
waft rhythm and blues across my tongue

You are my
sister
standing tall, strong, confident
who loves deeply--
her azure way
a bonfire blaze in my silver heart
rusty with thunder

## Far Away

Where the lapis sky meets the stars
where the village meets the valley
accumulated despair and love
filled the wellspring of the man ---
and rose like a cypress

The town is silent
indifferent
to that painting hand
while the heavens swirl and dance
blazing and twisting within itself
beautiful blend of turmoil and ecstasy

Now he is gone into the darkness
Now he is gone into a brilliant flash
joining the starry night

### *River Painting*

Winding through my heart
winding down, the river goes
winding past memories and they are
winding in my blood and I am
winding down the river road and it is
winding between hills and meadows and wildflowers
winding their way into the forest, turning and
winding back the hands of time
winding into my soul, the past when I was
winding my way through life and it was
winding its way into me and we were
winding together

## Where Are You Tonight

Where are you tonight
when the moon is full
the sky is naked
brandishing
leftover pebbles
tossed
waves quake
rim to rim
flood my sight with verdant blue

willow hanging its shroud
I peer beneath veil
for secrets
No   I'm only hiding
buried here I seek
lost memories
I forgot I had

trembling slightly in the cool air
I hear them rustle
scatter
are they afraid of me

## Shadows

Night encroaches
A covey of ravens
aim for the sunset moon
cross the moors
on satin black
cite omens
to shadows veiled in trees

shades of memories
flutter through tangled masses
echoes vibrate in an empty soul
wrenched and wretched minds twist
torn asunder by specters of speculation
trespassing
wreaking havoc

Hope clings
tenacious and tentative
falters
in a void filled with anguish
reaches to resurrection
on the soundless flight
of ebon wings

## *Scream*

A glimpse of screaming
Did you recognize…
      listen
      listen
Rage plain as welts
rises up
through a wailing wind
strains to break free
subtle simmer
seethes to a lathery boil
whispering in treetops
shrieking through the dark

## On the Edge

This knife so keen to
touch me
releases odor of sunlight
In the dark mirror
it whispers sweet nothings
reminiscent of lemon
I taste bitter dark chocolate
as it plunges
stirring my frosty ego
I hear it screaming
its stainless thin tongue
releasing words without vowels
resembling
the opera singer
her serrated voice cutting
harrowing keenly
shatters the looking glass

Reflected in its pieces
I gather the mosaic shards
to decorate my lofty castle

## *Mobius*

My cornerstone frayed ---
ripped from its moorings
I am set adrift--
away from the one anchor keeping me from falling off the end
into the still    deep waters
And I wonder if a haven will be found
sanctuary from this under-towing torrent
Elusive our ties

> Lives joined
> can be scattered
> by a zephyr passing
> Alone …. seeming forsaken
> I am empty
> grey


Your absence filled the well with tides of emotion
cast up flotsam that I scrawled among
poked at with my scrap of pencil
Gathering courage

> I cast a salvaged line
> hooked back in to our affinity

Encouragement entwined
through my life and yours
resurfaced

      By the light of your eyes
      essence of us stays
      I am
      boat to beacon
      moth to flame

### River I

River rages wild
leaping and gurgling
swirling silt through the body
through the soul
a fresh infusion of richness
swelling my heart
jumping for joy up the current
River takes my mind arcing
through the silvery air
flying through the mist
Full of life
waves rock
to sleep
the dreaming sand

## River II

River
part of my life
not forsaken

Loss of our language
feels like death

A shadow of your smell
whispered on the breeze
quickens my heart

Beneath the moon
too many changes

Your garden was my playground

My tiny will
boils sorrow
at your gate

### Sand Globe

Sand in glass globe
Thunder on mountain
River of life
rushes through my veins
opens pathways never tried

I look to you for comfort
lifeblood bringing
rich soil to my soul
making a place for regeneration and growth
cleansing
releasing sludge

Your unique odor
scent of water and moss and decay and sand and damp rocks
hot stones and dried wood
once heavy with water
rich with life and existence
constant
so essential to my dreams
your language a fading memory
misted by passage of time

I trudged your mud-lined shore

skipped stones off the top of your body --- it rippled with laughter

Saw other dreams pass by

watched as you carried mine

entwined

to ebb and flow with your whims of the day

Watched them

percolating  babbling  swirling


with sweet, distressful longing

I make pilgrimage to your shore


only to find a barrier

where none before existed


I can not touch you


Your essence remains

laced in my marrow

## *Lorelei*

Lorelei sings to my heart
river road sways
bank swirled with foggy mist
trees retreat up the hillside
disappear

I am lost in the mist which has risen to take your place in my heart
I am lost in the mist which has risen to swirl by the side of the river
I follow the narrow path
once clear and easy to see
now hidden by the swell of bushes
reaching into the core

the way your being
reached into the heart of my soul
now I go to the place once again
to find solace in a retreat
I am reclaiming

it will help be a salvation

against the arc of pain in my life that

threatens to keep me forever in its clutches

>How easy to intimidate a bond

>How much can be inflicted

>with a simple wave of a hand

>dismissing something unintentionally

>having no notion

>of what we have not said

## Tangible

I was tangible
but to you
a child of naught
a dust ball
who crawled
under the edge
of the cupboard
inconsequential piece of fluff
hidden
in the
wide open spaces
Unperceived
no encouragement offered
minimal courtesy call
       that's all


the kindred clan never looked

## *Abandoned*

You left me in ruins
An imploded structure
Walls stand bare
   exposed to the elements
   battered   buffeted
Gaping void
Hollow husk
Desolation
Windows bleak   vacant
Boarded over
No entrance      No exit
Piles of refuse
   both
   massively tangled   and
   wildly strewn
---those things we dare not touch--
   gather dust
   decay
            contaminate
Wind eddies through this cavern
Mournful bagpipes
   wailing through a shattered soul

### Silence Rings

Silence rings
iron-hued
through the night
Twilight
sparkles in a puddle
Waking oaks
dance with bended knee
wading among lupines
on the bank of the river
Gophers dream of darkness
their feet in rich, soft soil
Crickets pipe
tranquility
for
twitchy squirrel tails
River beckons all
to mist-shrouded quietness
reverberates
with the scent of life

### River Reel

River reels 'round
hides from humanity
as it meanders among the woods
I can't see it for the forest in my mind
which lets me in to retreat
from the
dampness and fog rising in a mist
that streams away as torrents retreat
from the gully of rapids washing over
into the drizzle of the waterfall arcing
over this maelstrom that threatens to negate
      with casual willfulness
the capricious current of ambition
swelled briefly
by a sprinkling
of complimentary precipitation

### *Frayed Hems*

I remember
frayed and basted hems
hair cut too short
or in need of one

stubby pencils
scrounged from the schoolyard

Sharp noises
Slammed doors
Hard voices
Whispers in my head
Names that were not mine
were not me
Too quiet silences

I remember
faded green house
surrounded by dirt and rocks

torn yellow curtains
small metal-framed bed
thin blankets
Cross above rickety dresser

Marbles in the dust
Stick boats floating in the ditch
Stunted patch of grass
in a hidden back corner
a flower in the neighbor's yard

### Fairy Tale

In the whirl
of
curses and ways
being hawked
still I expect a tower to arise
a fountain to reflect me
to fill my cup
with wondrous gifts
fill with light
balance with dark
top me off with
complexities and vagueness

Instead comes a tornado
I'm not where I was

I hear bells and whistles
but know it's just smoke
clouding visions
in the crystal ball

I hold in one hand
while the other inscribes token marks
upon a parchment
Images in an
unsheathed sword
transports me to a beautiful
forgotten realm of possibilities

here I find
a  pathway
and will look for my life
in these varied domains

## Normal

Tell me if I'm normal
Tell me if I'm blessed
Tell me if I'm crazy
Tell me if I'm depressed
Tell me if I'm lazy
Tell me if I'm right
Tell me if my apathy
is a symptom of my upbrung life
tell me if my wordlessness
         means there's something waiting inside
--or if I can't articulate
       the essence has practically died

Maybe buried under tons of rubble
an air-hole for to breathe
Or is it suffocated--
       and for it I should grieve

## Curiously Lazy

I am curious
I am lazy

looking for tidbits I
follow a branch
which forks   splits     divides
is part of
though far removed
from the original search

I may not have answered the original query
may have found much
or nothing pertaining to any need

a journey that perhaps taught me a little something
always worth the trip
the time
'cuz you just never know what might be found

## Absorption

A voice trickles in
rumbles low    distinct
like singed coffee
Strong words resonate
play into my subconscious
liquid crumbs
seeping in underneath

      Seasoned words tossed into the kettle
      it was your confounded recipes I would learn from
      Your status as salt of the earth
      heedlessly flung upon the ground
      where you expected things to grow

What form did you think your plantings would take
rashly sown with rotted roots
now that the soil is tilled
in salt-infused dirt
purifying in many ways        toxic in others

      Would the distress wash away in your lifetime?
      Let life grow unstunted?
      Too late

Renovation of the debilitated land
with encouragement of heartier fare to come
crumbles your word seeds--
to dry and die alone

       Condensation gathered brings
       life infusing dribbles
       soaked down into the hard-packed earth
       like sweet cream for coffee
       glorious drops of mist settles
       fanning embers for emboldenment

### Silent Stone

A voice comes from the silent stone she holds
And the drop of water it bleeds

She grinds it to powder
makes a gritty paste
paints words in the sand
with clay-glopped finger

Pulls algae from the river
wraps it around trees
marking passage
tucks leaves like messages in cracked bark

Turns over rocks and sticks
searching for pieces of herself under them
knowing she must
be here
somewhere

## No Longer Asks

She no longer asks for pieces of prose
for glimpses of spider shadows
roaming back alleys
questioning
dust bunny memories
fuzzy and unclear
gathering moss and twigs for nests
but never staying home

Aberrations roam
snaring the unwary thought
weaving tight while confidence no longer struggles
gathered strands lead     disjointed
back to the origin
while what should be passion
is buried

 the cracked structure
crumbles like old bricks
the rubble plundered
by repeated blows
of the wrecking ball

## Black

Black
depending
is all color
or none
the forest of your soul
is all colors
shapes   sizes
emptiness and fullness
At twilight
you are just beginning to form
into all you are
what in the light of day stayed shadowed
is now exposed
when you close your eyes
you can see deep inside the vastness
what you touch in the deepest reach of the abyss is obscure
but intense
there is an enduring center
which dislikes light
try a candle flame
and you may see authenticness lingering by the edge
you'll have to observe it without looking directly
it's watching you, too
it is hard to grab for an instant

let alone long enough to study it

lull it into a sense of security

you do not mean it any harm

indeed you do not

but it fears you

what you might do with it

it is often unsure itself

what the realistic honest precise pieces are

though all mingle to form full truth of self

and being insecure,  it is wary and shy

murkiness is its friend

as it has to be in neither world

there is no need to shift its stance

and that

is the best condition to catch it

just as the light is fading

or in the very late night hours

when it is tired of running around

it may even tell you a funny story

or shock you like ice water to the face

truth is cantankerous

## *If I Thought I Could*

If I thought I could
tell you everything
even those rambling
spiderweb thin connections
flitting   word   thought
leading to
deep down things
      if even I could find them
will I know when I finally
touch them
and not another tier of rose quartz
laid over the top
hiding and disguising truth
      would you listen to my journey

So long not saying
repressing   obscuring
      caution   always caution

Looking to explore the reservoir
clambering up walls

Only in my
      fleeting   [I]
            momentary   [do]
                 dreams   [tell you]

## *Words Rusty*

Words drop rusted flakes
brain creaks
groans
no doubt graphite is congealed
ink has leaked out
and only the work of fumbling fingers
profuse prodding
will restore
the fluid flow of prose

grease the gears
with books and coffee
music
fly the kite of imagination

put thoughts
    they sneak incognito
onto paper
with nobody the wiser
they decline
to disclose
what I thought
I was thinking

## *River Meets Soul*

River meets my soul
here at the bridge
here at the trickle
here where the rapids
flow into deep
and deep into swift
where the creek bed is dry
where birch trees snagged with leaves, moss and floundered twigs
       bind
       intertwine
irrevocably
tie us together
where rocks meet stones meet gravel meet sand meet silt
branches tossed join current
maybe later
the ocean
flat rocks meet farther bank
or hide mid-stream
here at edge of wet crust
where my hand
always reaches
to touch

### Terror of Waste

Terror of waste
yet we still
still
sad fool     sad fool
ignore disturbing things
they go away
then
you feel bereft     lonely
what
what if the shadows
never come back
they make you who you are
oh
there they are
waiting in darkness
in sunlight
tucked into inner caverns
ghostly things we keep
no blood, no guts
only unformed, scattered bones
we give life to
scratch and rattle when ignored too long
sorry we say
that other life took over

I am not afraid of you
but overwhelmed
unstructured myself
thankful for your generosity
all the fragments
you share
want to live with you so much
I forget
even a bit of time
is better than none
I should take
whatever time I have with you
I have skeleton keys
my father left me
let's see what we can unlock

## Where's the Kid

Where's the kid
who played at
being cowboy
batman     spiderman
those imaginary
inhabit some character game
where'd that stand up character go
Oh yeah
did that alone
no
comrade in arms
there were no buddies
switching roles
only blips of double scenes
figmental

no stage
no spotlight
no other eyes upon

now they watch
look at me
no     don't
oh please do

be polite
know you will
as shake in boots

trying to inhabit that
other
so you hear
could glimpse
the warrior

### What is Built Here

What is built here
a legacy of unrequited words
each shrouded in illusion
in evasion
normalcy

while my heart searches to prod me into passion
to follow the coursing smell of blue black rivers
to let the veins flow out

not resisting
not ignoring
the siren always sounding
beckoning
calling
warning

we have been a passive people
exploding inside
never in polite company

at night
in shadow
is boldness
alone beyond glaring light
where our feral side
does not fit

it would not do
to see the claws
in daylight

## *Unraveled*

Having lost the thread of conversation
amid wishes and waiting and past lives
she wonders what it all means
wandering around on these city streets
when she should have been a hermit
secluded away near a wide-open vista
mountains distant    blue

Now she's stuck here
mumbling along on the side
walking near the edge
looking for treasure in the canyons at her feet

Worn
tattered and torn
she carries a handful of blanket
like a scrap of love
bundled up
with woven fantasies
wrapped in gossamer
cobweb ends trailing behind

## Headlands Coffeehouse

I want to count the days
by the nights
spent at Headlands
drinking coffee
scribbling some lines
gazing down the alley
dreaming
music in the background
share a word or smile
with some stranger
feel part of
but so free to be
separate
centered
content enough
feel alive
feel home
leave happy
inspired
invigorated
to write
until the small hours

## Wild Things

Wild things
they used to have no leash
loping restlessly at night
sneaking down dirt alleys
stepping lightly on the gravel
hiding from those
who pursue
thinking to make them behave

They peer in a not-quite-closed curtain
just to see
roaming for the elusive prize
of finding self
already whole in the moment

Playing at unsophisticated nonsense
free to be wild
only partly human

Wild things
ran away
put on their boots and traveled far
took on the night

With nothing but a stick
and a knife
to keep claws sharp
went where they pleased

They had no tether
no fence
slowly constrained
captive now so long
seem only to remember darkness
but not how to live in it

Except
look now
is that a bit of furriness
is that a glint off fang

we are waiting
quietly howling and frenzied
for revival

## Day Done

Day is worn-out
as dusty froth gathers
a shimmer
a glimmer
a glint
and the chase is on
the hunt and seek and find
a quiet poke
follow a string sized trail
a whisper in the dark
is that my name I hear
heartbeat
I dare you
me    you dare me
who are you to taunt me
    a challenge it is
I am the flame which will burn you
I am life
cinders and ashes of that phoenix inside
this life keeps coming back
no matter that I think the spark has died

No      I arise

with two wings or one

shackled though I feel

still

the moon and sun rise and deep inside the flame resides

games me      it does

teases

waits until hope is shallow

a flare      a wisp

the prey flees and I follow

it courses

it hides

it runs again

I stalk

I pounce

take whatever scrap

wait quietly

oh so quietly

in the silence

it is mine

## Something in the Air

Something is in the air tonight
time stands still for a moment
leaps backward
falling over itself
keeping me awake
hovering here in silence
murmurs undercurrent
a soft white noise
holds time static

---

one light illumines darkness
marks no passage of hours
count to ten
count to three hundred
notice how many times
has tide changed
or is it the same interlude
over and over
illusion
wrapped in your own circle
it feels unaltered
but if this time is indistinguished
have you lost any
if it feels like before
is it

---

contained    embraced

does it hold you aloft

these odd moments mean so little

if you're unaware

it lingers

holds you dear

caresses

forgets you

left wondering

where you are

---

That whistle in your ear

is time rushing by

man made time

man made awareness

we are the only ones keeping track

nature is always present

measures it not

observes only this moment

looks not back

looks not forward

## *Prose Plight*

In eagerness and enthusiasm
stumbling occurs
words are clumsily toppled
off a tarnished tray
tumbling to the floor
landing embarrassed
in mixed-up heaps

scattered ones
scurry out of sight
hiding under well-wrought chairs
confused     scared
running together in jumbled packs
awaiting censorship of their behavior
fearing
their anxious wildness is not welcome

------ they'll get no blame from me--
letters symbols consonants vowels
'twas I who caused their downfall

all those words
some with skinned t's
marks of their essays into the wild
stream self-consciously into a corner

from the margin of the room
I invoke them to remain
the connotation of rapidly running words
a catharsis for my lost illusion
I offer them asylum
I let them free to do their verse

## Addicted to Words

I want to be addicted to words
sense flow
passion coursing
discover
use them      they use me
to welcome always
ink and paper and smell
emotion
heat and chill
vibration
I want to cry with them
play with them
drown myself with them
snatch from midnight air
their sound      fluttering
I am tired of ignoring
their plaintive wail
whimpering
I am tired of myself
treating them as
not belonging to me
as if they are less important
than others

I need them to be friends again
touch them
use the old
find new
integrate wholeness
take them on field trips
fulfill their wish to be heard
no longer dust covered reflections
afraid to be found
loving the dark
but seeking also the light
reserved creatures that they are
also desire spotlight
want to dance
under your eyes
across your mind
burrow in your thoughts
if only for a moment
if you welcome them to stay
so much the better
I want to pluck them from their silence
feed them blue blood
or red or black or rust

I want to pull
mine from me
to hold them
naked
raw
afraid
bold
fearless
ready to fight

I want them
to kick me in the ass
bind me to the chair
whip me till
I lose conscious thought
enter their world
rescue
define me
show me home

## *Thought Maybe Find Self*

Thought that maybe
I could find myself
if I went away

seems like the blues are here to stay
all the scattered-ness   confusion  came along anyway
but the farther I get
the more I smile
just don't look back

I know what's waiting far behind
piles of this   stacks of that
yeah don't worry, I'll be back
hour to hour    dragging my mind around
weighed down

I'll be alright
if I can drive all day
find some space
away from the pain
listening to my own voice
if only for awhile

### Messes of Words

Messes of words
piled here    there
bits scattered to the corners
unwritten
unspoken
writ by me
unspoken by me
unseen
I wish I had your strength
seem to have lost my own
thought I lost you, little ones
but here you are    thank you
we were to have a new home
space to run wild and free
you would have loved it
but no, not to be
we remain close cramped
imposed upon
I find so few ways to free us
I know I do not try hard enough
I am sorry
feel so pressed upon
we will be unshackled

## *Seemingly Haunted Woods*

Haunted woods
whisper my name
with a vulture's claw rasp

how could the sad spirits know my name

perhaps
because I planted the trees
watered the dark with
uncertainty
fear
what might have been

thoughts held in check
thoughts run amok

cloaked in normalcy

### *Fickle Finger*

This fickle finger fatefully frazzles
points that way
then this
stops giving directions
shifts to flashing
hey
oh never mind
wait   what   but
but I thought
I was doing this
oh come on it says
this is good for you
uh huh
I know your frivolous ways
lead me on then
change
throw up a slow  yield   no u-turn
stop sign
halt my progress
send in the mobius

## *Trouble Sleeping*

The problem
the trouble
of sleeping
is because
it is finally
quiet
surrounded by silence
not chaos
my mind likes to go out and play
in the street
the alley
go wandering to see what it can find
hopefully
get into trouble
make new friends
pouncing on this and that
like kitten
with bunch of new toys

### Turkey Vulture

I want to be a turkey vulture
pick at the essence
get all the scraps and snippets
dig in the nooks and crannies
for juicy morsels
kernels
excavating
stretching tendrils
lingering over ligaments
when harvested all I can
from appendages
from the quarry
uncovered
preponderance of parts
I will lay out the prolific miscellany
which
forms the motley mosaic
of my life

## Curve of River

Curve of river
stony on my side
dead end road
three concrete steps to
powdery narrow expanding to wide dirt path
beach opens before you
soft sandy to rock
to muck to water
smell of dead life
new life
BB rifle
sticks tossed
stones skipped
pollywogs
willow and birch
eight foot aluminum boat
silence as float
Fitch to Memorial
 Asti to Fitch
line in water
cast and retrieve
his white high-top tennis shoes
my blue ones

## *Merging*

With dust on bodies
earth on hands
we come to renew our lives
carrying hopes
dreams for selves and children
leaving old countries for new
bringing skills, learning others
to do our best, hard work
coming through Nova Scotia, Mexico,
from lands far away
forsaking homelands
for opportunity
sharing our cultures
blending
becoming American

### *Tired he is*

Tired
he is
of the boring
but he loves the parts
the pieces
that make the whole
good at figuring puzzles
filling holes
in others lives
making complete
out of broken bits

struggles though
to patch
own empty spots
but there are no
codes
diagrams
maps
for that

## Zookiness

If I had but known
I would have wandered through my garden patch
looking to the zuchs for guidance
I would have taken time to sow seeds of zooky thought
onto damp paper pieces
watched as they sprouted with life
the way lima beans grew
on brown fiber towels in first grade
I would have followed tendrils of thought to the end of
       their conclusions
wandering off among hither and yon paths
as they are so wont to do
I would have sat by their side
watching as they burst forth from yellow flower into tiny,
       tender beings
hovered anxiously as they started for adult zucchini-ness
then been amazed at the giant spurt into full zucchini-hood
the moment I left their side
as they threaten to dispatch all others in the area
Zuc-a-ninny my father might have called them
but I have yet to meet a stupid or silly one
and their patience when used for boating or racing or a doll has yet
       to be surpassed

Ah, the proud zook!

Though we boil it and fry it and shred it and dip it into all sorts
    of things

still it is willing to return every year into our gardens and kitchens

thriving in escalating growth

so as to be lovingly shared with all people

both those who are our neighbors

and with our most fleeting acquaintances

as in our hearts we are moved by the zuchs' generosity

and prolific product

to be so likewise generous to folks around us

and we must remember

as we go about our daily lives

that a zucchini by any other name

may be a summer squash

### Changes

Wonder what happened

moved away      searching

knew it would cause you despair

but had to try

moved back north

got hellish job

finally made contact

I see you

felt like twenty years not gone

but now

different

I couldn't answer right

you stepped even further away

I couldn't reach you

you would not let me

When your world

was in doubt

you reached out

I did what I could

apprehensive, I could not open arms

      catch glimpse of you

      now and then

      but you aren't here

## 'Big Man'

Can identify
   just a bit
with your big man
Thank you
for giving him freedom to
rage
vent
be physical
to purge
anger
hopelessness
his downtrodden feelings
his hiding against
any show of emotion
so all that's left on top
is appearance of rage
For seeing his heart
his love
his actual caring
his gentle core
that scared of his own self
that protects his six year old inside

## *Not Dreaming*

The inspiration for this poem came from Anna Nalick's song "Consider This" on her album *Wreck of the Day* (2004).


I'd rather not dream
that I'm well-adjusted
but I will be okay
I'll tell you my falterings
if you may ask
then we can let it go

I'd rather be present as allowed
than hide in the corner
being invisible

I'd rather let you think
I might be even odder than you
'cause you might be right
and that's got to be okay

I'd rather
as John Wooden said
"Do not let what you cannot do
interfere with what you can do"
so am trying

I'd rather try walking through this fire
whistle as I burn
they can't get you if you whistle or hum

Facing down the demons
because inside
I am that strong
no matter what synapses try to fool me with

I can temper their influence
with a little help
ignore the fact
that they could still drop me to my knees
if they gang up and ambush

then the fight is not pretty

pushing the comfort zone
but then, I used to walk the streets alone at night
I drive miles and states alone
though that is not the same as participating

I do not have to be well-adjusted
present a pretty picture to the masses
never have been
though wanted to fit in a little better
why should
 I
start now

it's my bubble wrap
and my ledge

## Sits on Couch

She sits on the couch
hands clasped behind her neck
gazing out the window
at a field far away
      through the bleak rain

In the mirror she sees illusion
distinctive delusion
simulation for others
façade of faux
face of fiction

In the parking lot she sits
arms resting on the steering wheel
it rains harder
drops fall off the tree
ping-pong balls
onto a metal table

Wants to write about real life
but doesn't think it's hers
doesn't think she knows what it is
thinks she's not part of it

Wants to write about someone she loves
can't get inside to reach that essence
can't find the image

She is afraid the well of words she believes exists
to be nothing but a mirage
to be just another part of her vague life
is afraid to not find honest words
is afraid she'll never get through the wall
is afraid to try
is afraid not to try
knows not trying is already failing
is afraid of the pain she might find
when she reaches for the truth
afraid no pain found
is afraid not reaching deep enough
will destroy her

But the anger is real
depression
angst
disquiet

apathy

emotion

distress

disturbance

pain

depth

the silence is real

      the words are far too simple

      the explanations, the excavations

      not deep enough


Somewhere in her hands lays the answer

Somewhere in her mind lies the truth

Somewhere in the heart screams swallowed dreams

Somewhere in the dark she lets it loose

## Rocks and Water

She looks at
rocks and water
for an answer

pieces of junk
broken things

can they crack open
her soul
release heart

raises hand to moon
but it's not talking

listens to the stream
walks the streets

turns music up
turns down
'cuz doesn't need
no extra words in her head

rolls down the truck window
drives for hours

gets some dirt on her boots
looking for gold
in ripples of creek
and adopted stones

### *Pungent Dusk*

Pungent dusk
muck at water's edge
moss fresh
  where river slips up to taste
sun-baked algae
crumbling residue
  where puddles have shrunk
scent of
wet autumn leaves
swirled into heaps
fermented by harvest moon
sediment marked trees
copses hunched and knotted
against last winter's deluge

Why does the river
take my tears
it already
has my heart

## Born Here

I was born here
skinned my knees
on your Mountaineers playground
rode my bike to get comics
at Redwood
the plaza grocery
to get ice cream
Ben Franklin's Five and Dime
for toys
the Bakery
for apple turnovers
never once locking it


rode up the Avenue
past small orchards of plums
past Packers and Canners grocery

I walked after school
from Powell
on University or Fitch or Center
to home
more than a mile between
with no thoughts of fear

I was a few years younger
than the neighbor boy
but we
caught bees in jars
broke rocks to see inside
popped red strips of cap gun powder
went up by the railroad tracks
where I sometimes picked white stones
to give to my mother
played around the Sunsweet boxes
piled high in the lot at Mill Street

One day
        after climbing back down
        from the roof of the machine shop
        across the street
we started tossing rocks at each other
just because
[I may have started it]
I ended up with four stitches
but it missed my left eye

My father and I fished at Basalt
below the dam

took float trips
on his eight foot aluminum boat
down from Camp Rose to Memorial
Alexander Valley to Fitch Mountain

I went to his work
at Idaco Lumber
to my mother's
at Cottage Café

The fire station
was still on Center
Police station on the corner
Greyhound station diagonal

Then we lived on the mountain
and I spent
days and hours
alone on the edge of the river
there my soul stays

I was born here

## Scars

We wear our scars
upon our arms
hide their origin
hide their reality
inner torment surfacing
violence anger frustration
       rising like one-toed bird tracks
sometimes just because
sometimes we just like it
the way it looks
experiment with different designs
you may see my tattoo
but I don't do it for you
An adult   do as you please
Ha
people still watch
creativity limited by society acceptance
not allowed
       must be some problem   real problem   trouble
       we must find it and fix it
       can't have you doing that now can we
we want to observe you
question you

help you
leave me alone
I can't explain   I won't explain
none of your business
I ain't bothering anyone
banshee screams are reverberating

the tenacious grip
occasionally loosens more

hold me
but don't touch me
let the inner become outer
let it purge
primal express
don't run away
but let me be
resist against invisible bonds

## Allusion

Your soft warm fingers
meander
break the surface
meld into my being
become part of me
yet you remain separate

laying beside me
your body warms in the sun
when you become too hot
I send chills up your spine
take off the edge
release the flush of heat

you submerge with me
swirl round and round
gently
I flow with you
around you
over you

you doze in the shade
I murmur a rapid little tune
wait for you to
come play again
come to the edge
dive in

## The Block

This writer's block feels like a void

filling with fog so thick the sun can't shine  [oh that is so clichéd]

I search for another word in the dark  [clichéd again]

I search for a word in the murk  [not quite so bad]


A word

is a single word, any word, many words, enough to illumine any
thought that streaks or slugs by the malfunctioning thought process


Whither hast thou goest; enthusiasm, esteem, fervor ?

It seems that with no water in the bath, the birds and dragonflies
do not come with tidbits and bright pieces to dress the imagination,
and this book before me promises something to happen -- but not,
perhaps, for days-- that is, for noon-nights, when I toil the best. Or
maybe that is toil the beast. Though sometimes the beast is a thing
of beauty  [oh clichéd again]  Ah, and we all know how the beautiful
thing we think we know can be the most beastly of all


So I kept hope that suddenly words would pour forth freely, the
lead in my pencil turning to molten,  the ink in my pen flowing like
a crick, I mean creek, onto the paper, forming wonderful words in
sublime script


Or maybe phrases would ooze from my pores, that I might pluck
them off my skin, off my sleeve, fresh from my heartsoil -- and form
them into place with hands of grace and wisdom, to produce a few
lines worthy of my humble merit

But alas, I lack the vision, the music, which glows out of the darkness. That darkness within, without which I may not sleep the dreams of muted glory. So once more into the fray, with a sometimes 'fraid and frayed mind, which may not be up to code, but I call it home

### I Know Words

Words
sometime seem
like merely sounds
thoughts voiced are
not of substance

when spoken
float away    or
crash to the ground

it is hard to convey
with my meager selection

what I want the words to carry
what I want the words to
mean
don't always equal what you hear
I see they are not having connotations
delivering my thoughts
right images
to the person I am speaking with

but in that moment
can't find a way to
correct the error
change the equation
so it speaks equally to us both

[sometimes they just will not let you clarify]

## Hard to Sow

It is hard to sow
then having sown
wonder just what it is you planted
what you will reap
        you are supposed to sow    .
        without wondering at the results

but I think most would like some feedback
some idea what type of plant
has been pushed into the soil
is it fertile    barely alive    barren
if we sow to soil which had no interest
first try a bit more water
if no growth
we need to move on
no point in tending to that which appears to not be wanted
but still toss a few seeds onto that soil
because you just never know
often seeds lie dormant
waiting
suddenly take root
accepting changes

## *Hear Me Screaming*

Why don't you hear me
screaming
don't you look at
       listen

       listen

       listen
can you not see below the mildness
my rage is as plain
as the scars
on my body
break free   break free
I have no voice
       I must scream
I am not a bottle
to hold things
stuffed in me
keeping the cork in
I am a teapot
whistling   shrieking
as the insides simmer
then boil

## Not of this Body

I am not of this body
I stand to one side
barely a participant
like being involved with a character
in a movie
watching from a not quite intimate position
involved with the character on the screen
seeing    feeling with them
        but not of them
I am outside myself as I watch them
a feeling often with me
apart
enclosed in glass walls
of house and auto
looking through windows of coffee shops
looking out from somewhere behind my eyes
I see parts of the world go by
and wonder
if I'll ever be in it
        again

was I ever
if I was
distance has grown farther

I have no distinct memory
when was I
and not only
standing offside
watching the chaos of families
interaction
how does that feel within

### Water Flurries

Water flurries whipped by the wind
swirl     dance
with leaves in the courtyard

ushering in
their brothers arrival
magnitude increasing
like the Billy Goats Gruff

arriving
to drown our drought
quench its thirst

showing a fraction of power
rain pummels the ground
causes mild floods
enhances erosion
of bricks and concrete
power to destroy
power to nurture
intertwines with each other
thunderstorm

## *River Percolates*

River percolates
through my blood
seeps into whirlpools
eddies
my Don Quixote heart
resides in deep pockets along the edge
drifts past memories
resting on the bank
interspersed
like discarded rusting automobiles
sometimes I trawl for
thoughts
flow past like flotsam
I lure them out to take a better look
gently toss them back into the river
 my home where I may not live

## MLC

In the death we have here
I no longer can find you
vanished
no trace
I left with no goodbye
we both scattered
lost you
in time
I search
too vast
the space you may occupy
I wish we had not left it
hanging so
I take blame
life so odd then
I apologize
I'd like to
but never explained
so convoluted and weird
vanished
we were gone
thirty years later
still wonder how you are

your life

where are you

are you well

I look and see no trace

even old and faint

married now

you might be

perhaps out of area

out of state

------

I've been haunting all the café's

you went to

see if you might

be inside

one of those odd things I do

don't I know it

but lately you've been

so much on my mind

    I don't know why

a strange thing

yes I know

but

was that perhaps

one of the things
you liked
so
I keep hoping
after all of this
time
has gone
I keep anticipating
optimistic cynic that I am
I may find you
see if we're still
friends
 much as we ever were
I stayed away
you moved
haven't seen you since
our lives diverged
not enough words
I had no voice
now you're nowhere to be found
I have no choice
no way to say hello
no way to reconnect

about how our lives

went

so I keep hoping

every now and again

going over the same old ground

where there's been no trace of you before

but got to try

just once more

maybe you'll step out

of the car parked next to mine

then we'll see

are we still friendly

or maybe don't even remember

I know you're out there somewhere

thirty years have passed

but it feels

so recent sometimes

memories stick in the time that they happen

I'm still out here

hoping we connect

put our changed selves

to the test

I know we're

somewhere

are you still waiting tables
are you serving at a bar
maybe doing real estate
studied law
moved back to Vegas
where tips are better
take up photography
did your mom pass away on you
did your sister go to jail
has your son made you proud
do you wish your daddy knew
still drink Black Russians
go out to the park
John and his Bronco still around
you go out to the beach

go back to school
write a book
work at a winery
bet you still stand strong

## Acknowledgments

Thanks to the Healdsburg Literary Guild salon
for letting me share my words.
Even though each reading disquiets me
it also reassures me.

Previously published works include:

*River Stone* and *Silent Stone*
in *Healdsburg and Beyond!*, a 2015 Healdsburg
Literary Guild publication.

*Merging* in the *Russian River Recorder* (Fall 2015–Issue 130), a
publication of the Healdsburg Museum.

Other poems in *Healdburg Haiku*,
a chapbook publication of the Literary Arts Council.

## *Poet's Biography*

Karen Hayes spent her early years in Healdsburg, California,
where she whiled away several formative years entertaining herself
along the bank of the Russian River on Fitch Mountain.

She currently lives in Sonoma County and loves to spend her
vacation time in Ft. Bragg in northern California,
where she gets most of her writing done.

She was an original participant in the Literary Arts Council
of the Healdsburg Arts Council.

www.ingramcontent.com/pod-product-compliance
Lightning Source LLC
Chambersburg PA
CBHW060812050426
42449CB00008B/1641